Goodness Me
it's
Gluten Free

By Mary & Vanessa Hudson

Copyright © 2012 Goodness Me Limited,

Tauranga, New Zealand

www.goodnessme.co.nz

Published By: Goodness Me Limited
First Edition 2012

Photography, Design, Text: All copyright © 2012
Mary & Vanessa Hudson

Copy Editor: Jill Hudson

Cover Photo: Lemon Meringue Pie
by Vanessa Hudson

ISBN: 978-0-473-22065-5

A CIP catalogue record for this book is available from the National Library of New Zealand.

All rights reserved. No part of this publication may be reproduced, stored in a retrieval system, or transmitted in any form, or by any electronic means, photocopied, recorded or otherwise reproduced without the prior written permission of copyright owner.

All the recipes in this book have been carefully tested by Mary & Vanessa Hudson who along with the publisher have made every effort to ensure that the instructions are accurate and safe, but they cannot accept liability for any resulting injury or loss or damage to property, whether direct or consequential.

Contents

Introduction	5
Before You Begin Baking	6
Conversion Tables	7
Goodness Me Flour Blends	8
Allergies & Intolerances	9
Biscuits & Cookies	11
Cakes & Slices	21
Breads	35
Muffins & Scones	49
Pastry, Pikelets & Pancakes	61
Recipe Index	79

Introduction

If you've picked up this book it's likely that you or someone you know has been diagnosed as Coeliac or is choosing to eat gluten free. Often this diagnosis brings with it feelings of despair, as it seems as if all the foods you once used to enjoy eating are now off limits to you, especially baked goods like bread, pies, pastry, cakes, and cookies. Well, not anymore! We have packed this book full of easy to bake, delicious gluten free food so that you can once again satisfy the simple pleasure of eating food that is a delight to the taste buds. We have decided not to spend time educating you about the ins and outs of being gluten intolerant/Coeliac as there are many other books and websites available that already serve that purpose, but instead focus on baking the food itself.

Rest assured we have been where you are, we are a mother and daughter whose family first encountered the need to eat gluten free because of a Coeliac diagnosis more than 12 years ago, and the subsequent discovery that in fact three quarters of our family were affected with varying degrees of gluten intolerance. As you can imagine, this diagnosis threw our family's eating habits into chaos. Everywhere we shopped was an array of foods that we could no longer eat, a simple trip to a café was filled with frustration, and packed lunches... well, who could stomach the thought of the crumbly, cardboard or brick like, gluten free "bread" that was on offer? Not us! We briefly entertained the idea of a lifetime of denial and avoidance of gluten containing foods, but being foodies at heart we were not content to simply give up eating the things we loved. So we embarked on a quest to create delicious, satisfying, gluten free baked goods that are as much of a joy to cook as they are to eat.

We started by developing a decent sized loaf of bread that could be made into sandwiches, and with this success we launched Goodness Me Ltd and sold our bread mixes through our website www.goodnessme.co.nz. Meanwhile we continued our experimentation and soon to follow was a crêpe, waffle and baking mix. As the years have passed gluten free flours have become readily available to everyone, not just food manufacturers, in supermarkets and shops, so we decided it was time to create a Goodness Me cookbook to share the secrets of our gluten free bread and baking mixes and the large collection of recipes we've developed.

It is our desire that everyone will be able to easily and successfully recreate these recipes even someone who has never baked before. To help, we've ensured the recipe instructions cover the basics and a realistic photo accompanies each recipe. We hope you will enjoy the satisfaction that comes from baking and, of course, eating fantastic, tasty and visually appealing gluten free food as much as we do. If you have any doubts that this cookbook is for you, the fact that "we eat what we bake" should give you the confidence that these recipes are so good your friends will want to know what your secret is!

After all: "Life's too short to eat terrible food".

Before You Begin Baking

We want you to enjoy baking as much as we do, and so have made this book as easy to follow as possible. We enjoy baking in a home environment (not a commercial kitchen) and so take a creative rather than precise approach to our cooking. This means that when the recipes give you a measurement such as 1 cup of something we expect you to just scoop a cup of the ingredient out of, say, your bulk **Baking Blend** container and shake off excess instead of using a knife to level the top. Same with spoon measurements. One reason we bake this way which maybe contrary to how you have been taught, is that we have found there is some variability in the flours available in the store and so one batch of **Baking** or **Bread Blend** may differ from another to a certain degree. So have fun with your baking, relax, get the measurements close to what the recipe requires but don't stress with having cups and spoons perfectly levelled off.

So many things can affect how a recipe will turn out, such as variability in your raw ingredients, your oven etc, so embrace the experiment and if the recipe is not how you expect it to turn out the first time then make some adjustments to how you did it and have another go. Using gluten free flours is quite different to "normal" flour so if you are used to baking with "normal" flours then the mixtures in this book will have different textures (wetter or drier, depending on the recipe) than you might expect, but this is ok.

Measuring Cup & Spoons:

These recipes were developed using New Zealand standard metric culinary measures. Which for your reference are 1 cup = 250ml, 1 Tablespoon = 15ml and 1 teaspoon = 5ml. However, because we have used cup and spoon sizes in our recipes where possible (rather than weight - with the exception of butter), then whatever the standard culinary cups and spoons are in your country (providing you use the same utensils throughout the recipe thus keeping the proportions the same) you should produce a similar result as using New Zealand culinary measures. So use what you have and get baking. Culinary measuring cups & spoons mean the sort used for baking as pictured, which can usually be found as sets quite cheaply in the utensil aisle of your local supermarket. Don't use the spoons from your cutlery drawer. These are quite different in size.

Weight Conversions as used for Butter

Metric Weights	Imperial Baking Weights (have been rounded)
25g	1oz
50g	2oz
75g	2¾oz
100g	3½oz
125g	4oz
150g	5oz
200g	7oz
250g	9oz
500g	1lb 2oz
1kg	2lb

Oven Temperature Conversions

Celsius	Fahrenheit	Gas Mark
150°C	300°F	2
170°C	325°F	3
180°C	350°F	4
190°C	375°F	5
200°C	400°F	6
220°C	425°F	7
230°C	450°F	8

Ovens: The oven we used when test baking the recipes is a 3 year old domestic oven with fan bake/fan forced capabilities. Your oven may be very different and some adjustments will need to be made to the temperatures and cooking times stated in the recipes to suit your particular oven. Generally speaking if you don't have a fan bake/fan forced option, add 5 - 10 minutes to the cooking time, or approx. 10°C to the temperature, possibly both if your oven is older. You will need to experiment. For standard temperature conversions see chart above.

Abbreviations: We have tried to keep these to a minimum to make the recipes easier to follow. To avoid confusion measurements listed as 1½ cups mean 1 cup plus another ½ cup and so on.

About Gums: We have used guar gum in these recipes. We have found there is little difference between xanthan and guar gum but when substituting xanthan for guar gum usually half the amount of xanthan gum is sufficient to produce the same results. If you use a different gum you will need to experiment to find the best proportion for these recipes.

Goodness Me Flour Blends

We have created two flour blends for use in our recipes, **Baking Blend** for all the baking and **Bread Blend** for bread. Our blends use whole grains as much as possible ensuring they have a higher fibre and nutritional content, as well as being lower GI, than most commercially available blends. The gluten free flours we use for our blends should be readily available at your local supermarket, bulk bin store, ethnic or whole foods market. For convenience, the blends make a larger quantity than you need for a single recipe so that you can keep the rest in your store cupboard and when the inspiration strikes, you can just scoop out a cupful and get baking.

We don't want to bore you with the scientific reasoning behind how gluten works and why gluten free flours are different, and why we chose the flours we did for our blends (aside from the health benefits already mentioned), as although this can be fascinating it's not the purpose of this book. However if you do want to learn more about the different flours we use our website www.goodnessme.co.nz has further information.

As there are no preservatives in the blend, the shelf life will be the same as labelled on the individual flours. The blend is best kept in a sealed storage container in a cool dry place. Also check the labels in store when buying each individual flour to make sure it has been manufactured according to gluten free standards.

To make either of the blends below, only use one set of measurements e.g. only metric or only imperial don't mix the two. After measuring out the blend ingredients into a large container, be sure to thoroughly mix the flours together before using in the recipes.

Baking Blend

Makes 1.3kg (3lb)
300g (12oz) Fine Rice Flour
400g (14oz) Buckwheat Flour
600g (1lb 5oz) Fine Maize Flour

Bread Blend

Makes 3 loaves or 2.3kg (5lb) flour
9 cups or 1280g (2lb 12oz) White Rice Flour
3 cups or 390g (14oz) Buckwheat Flour
3 cups or 300g (12oz) Maize Flour or Polenta
3 cups or 330g (12oz) Tapioca Flour/Starch

Maize flour can be named or labelled in many different ways and can be made with maize or corn, but it is always **yellow.** The white maize cornflour commonly used for thickening sauces works differently in recipes because it is 100% starch, so please don't use it in the Goodness Me flour blends. If you can't tolerate or don't want to use fine maize flour, it can be successfully substituted for the same weight of sorghum flour. The fine maize flour used in the **Baking Blend** can also be used for the **Bread Blend** though the coarser maize flours like polenta do give a nice texture in bread. If you like a denser and more wholegrain loaf of bread you can substitute the white rice flour for the same weight of brown rice flour or add 1 cup of rice bran when making the blend.

Allergies & Intolerances

All the recipes, Baking and Bread Blends are free from:
- Gluten, Wheat, Potato, Soy, and Nut flours

Dairy Free: All our **bread** recipes are dairy free, but only some of our baking recipes are. We have used butter in many of our baking recipes as dairy intolerance isn't the focus of this book. We encourage you to experiment by substituting the butter with oil or dairy free spread if you like.

Egg Free: You may have your own preferred egg substitute, but we have found the following one works well in the **bread** recipes, and may also work well in other recipes though we have not tested it there.
1. Grind to a powder 3 Tablespoons of whole flax seed (linseed).
2. Pour over this 9 Tablespoons of boiling water.
3. Leave for about 15 minutes to activate and then use in place of the eggs in the **bread** recipes.
4. Please note if using, you will need to reduce the total water in the bread recipe by a ¼ cup.

Baking Powder and Icing Sugar: These are not always gluten free so read the label when purchasing to ensure you buy only products that are gluten free.

Biscuits & Cookies

Irresistible Chocolate Chip Cookies 12

Dainty Biscuits 13

Cherry & Coconut Cookies 14

Cranberry Cookies 15

Coconut Crunch Cookies 16

Afghan Cookies 17

Gingernutty Cookies 18

Oodles Cookies 19

Walnut Creams 20

Irresistible Chocolate Chip Cookies

Ingredients:

2 cups **Baking Blend** (p.8)
½ teaspoon baking soda
½ teaspoon salt
1 cup soft brown sugar
¼ cup white sugar
1 teaspoon vanilla essence
1 egg
175g butter (melted)

1 cup chocolate chips

Method:

1. Turn oven on to 170°C fan bake.
2. Prepare up to 3 baking trays by covering with baking paper.
3. Put the first 7 ingredients into a large bowl (**Baking Blend**, soda, salt, sugars, vanilla & egg).
4. Mix through with a fork.
5. In a pot melt the butter and then add this to the large bowl and mix everything together well.
6. Lastly, add the chocolate chips to the cookie dough and mix through thoroughly to evenly distribute. Spoon in small teaspoon sized lots onto the prepared baking trays, allowing enough room between each cookie for it to spread to double its size while cooking.
7. Bake at 170°C fan bake for 12 - 15 minutes until golden brown.
8. Remove from oven and transfer to wire rack to cool.
9. Repeat steps 7 - 9 until all the cookie dough used up.
10. When cold, store in **airtight** tin. These cookies can keep for weeks but are so irresistible they don't usually last that long.

Tip: Be careful to let your cookie dough cool slightly before adding the chocolate chips or they will start to melt and discolour the biscuits.

This recipe makes a lot of cookies.

Dainty Biscuits

Ingredients:

75g butter (softened)
½ cup soft brown sugar
¼ cup castor sugar
1 egg
1 teaspoon vanilla essence
1 cup **Baking Blend** (p.8)
1 teaspoon baking powder
Pinch salt

Red berry jam
e.g. strawberry

Method:

1. Preheat oven to 190°C fan bake.
2. In a large bowl, using an electric beater, beat together the butter and sugars until smooth and creamy.
3. Add in the egg and vanilla and beat again.
4. Mix in all the dry ingredients until well combined (not the jam).
5. Prepare a baking tray by greasing or covering with baking paper.
6. Place teaspoonfuls of the cookie dough onto a cold baking tray.
7. Make a small indent with the handle of a teaspoon in the top of each biscuit on the tray and place ¼ teaspoon of jam into each one.
8. Bake at 190°C fan bake for 12 - 15 minutes until golden brown.
9. Remove biscuits from the tray and cool on a wire rack.
10. When cold, store in **airtight** tin.

Cherry & Coconut Cookies

Ingredients:

75g butter (softened)
½ cup soft brown sugar
¼ cup castor sugar
1 egg
1 teaspoon vanilla essence
1 cup **Baking Blend** (p.8)
1 teaspoon baking powder
Pinch salt
½ cup chopped glace cherries
(cut cherries into 4)
½ cup coconut

Method:

1. Preheat oven to 190°C fan bake.
2. In a large bowl, using an electric beater, beat together the butter and sugars until smooth and creamy.
3. Add in the egg and vanilla and beat again.
4. Then mix in all remaining ingredients.
5. Prepare a baking tray by greasing or covering with baking paper.
6. Place teaspoonfuls of the cookie dough onto a cold baking tray.
7. Bake at 190°C fan bake for 12 - 15 minutes until golden brown.
8. Remove cookies from tray and cool on a wire rack.
9. When cold, store in **airtight** tin.

Tip: Make these an almond biscuit by replacing the cherries with roughly chopped almonds.

Cranberry Cookies

Ingredients:

75g butter (softened)
½ cup soft brown sugar
¼ cup castor sugar
1 egg
1 teaspoon almond essence
1 cup **Baking Blend** (p.8)
1 teaspoon baking powder
Pinch salt
½ cup dried cranberries

Method:

1. Preheat oven to 190°C fan bake.
2. In a large bowl, using an electric beater, beat together the butter and sugars until smooth and creamy.
3. Add the egg and almond essence and beat again.
4. Mix in all dry ingredients and cranberries.
5. Prepare baking trays by greasing or covering with baking paper.
6. Place teaspoonfuls of the cookie dough onto a cold baking tray.
7. Bake at 190°C fan bake for 12 - 15 minutes until golden brown.
8. Remove cookies from tray and cool on a wire rack.
9. When cold, store in **airtight** tin.

Coconut Crunch Cookies

Ingredients:

75g butter (softened)
½ cup soft brown sugar
¼ cup castor sugar
1 egg
1 teaspoon vanilla essence
1 cup **Baking Blend** (p.8)
1 teaspoon baking powder
Pinch salt
½ cup coconut
½ cup cornflakes (crushed)

Method:

1. Preheat oven to 190°C fan bake.
2. Prepare baking tray by greasing or covering with baking paper.
3. In a large bowl, using an electric beater, beat together the butter and sugars until smooth and creamy.
4. Add the egg and vanilla and beat again.
5. Add all the remaining ingredients and mix well.
6. Place cookie dough in small teaspoon sized lots on a cold baking tray.
7. Bake at 190°C fan bake for 12 - 15 minutes until golden brown.
8. Remove cookies from tray and cool on a wire rack.
9. When cold, store in **airtight** tin.

Afghan Cookies

Ingredients:

200g butter (softened)
¾ cup sugar
1¼ cups **Baking Blend** (p.8)
3 Tablespoons cocoa powder
1 cup cornflakes (crushed)

Icing Ingredients:

2 Tablespoons cocoa powder
1 Tablespoon boiling water
2 cups icing sugar
Walnut or pecan halves

Method:

1. Preheat oven to 180°C fan bake.
2. Prepare baking tray by greasing or covering with baking paper.
3. In a large bowl, using an electric beater, beat together the butter and sugar until smooth and creamy.
4. Add the **Baking Blend**, cornflakes and cocoa powder.
5. Press together in Tablespoon sized lots then roll into balls and place on a baking paper covered baking tray.
6. Press cookie dough balls lightly with your hand to flatten.
7. Bake at 180°C fan bake for 12 - 15 minutes.
8. Cool on the tray for a few minutes then transfer to a wire rack to finish cooling.
9. When cold, ice with chocolate icing.
10. Make icing in a small bowl by dissolving cocoa powder in boiling water, then add icing sugar and mix until smooth.
11. Ice the cookies, then decorate with a walnut or pecan half before icing sets.
12. Store in **airtight** tin.

Gingernutty Cookies

Ingredients:

125g butter (softened)
½ cup soft brown sugar
3 Tablespoons golden syrup

1 teaspoon baking soda
1 Tablespoon boiling water

1¼ cups **Baking Blend** (p.8)
Pinch salt
2 teaspoons powdered ginger
2 teaspoons root ginger
(finely grated)

Method:

1. Preheat oven to 180ºC fan bake.
2. Prepare baking tray by greasing or covering with baking paper.
3. In a large bowl, using an electric beater, beat together the butter, sugar and golden syrup until smooth and creamy.
4. In a small bowl/cup dissolve the baking soda in the water, then add this to the large bowl along with the rest of the ingredients. Mix well.
5. Roll teaspoonful sized lots of cookie dough into balls and place on cold baking tray.
6. Press with a damp fork in both directions to make a crisscross pattern.
7. Bake at 180ºC fan bake for 12 - 15 minutes until golden brown.
8. Remove from tray and cool on a wire rack.
9. When cold, store in **airtight** tin.

Oodles Cookies

Ingredients:

1 cup sugar
250g butter
3 Tablespoons golden syrup
1 teaspoon baking soda
3 cups **Baking Blend** (p.8)

Method:

1. Turn oven on to 160°C fan bake.
2. Prepare up to 3 baking trays by covering with baking paper.
3. In a saucepan melt together butter, sugar, golden syrup and baking soda until the sugar is dissolved.
4. Remove from the heat and add 3 cups of **Baking Blend**.
5. Mix well.
6. Place teaspoonfuls of the cookie dough 10cm apart, on a cold baking tray.
7. Bake first tray at 160°C fan bake for 10 minutes.
8. Prepare the next tray while the first batch of cookies are baking.
9. Leave baked cookies on the baking tray for a few minutes to 'set' before transferring to a wire rack to cool.
10. Then repeat steps 6 - 9 until all dough is used up.

Tip: These cookies got their name because the dough makes oodles and oodles of cookies.

Walnut Creams

Ingredients:

75g butter (softened)
½ cup soft brown sugar
¼ cup castor sugar
1 egg
1 teaspoon vanilla essence
1 cup **Baking Blend** (p.8)
1 teaspoon baking powder
Pinch salt
1 cup walnuts (chopped)

Walnut pieces for topping (optional)

Method:

1. Turn oven on to 190°C fan bake.
2. In a large bowl, using an electric beater, beat together the butter and sugars until smooth and creamy.
3. Add the egg and vanilla and beat again.
4. Mix in all the dry ingredients including chopped walnuts.
5. Prepare baking trays by greasing or covering with baking paper.
6. Place small teaspoonfuls of the cookie dough onto a cold baking tray.
7. Press a walnut piece into the top of each cookie if using.
8. Bake at 190°C fan bake for 12 - 15 minutes until golden brown.
9. Remove from tray and cool on a wire rack.
10. When cold, store in **airtight** tin.

Cakes & Slices

Carrot Cake 22

Banana Cake 23

Moist Fruit Cake 24

Christmas Cake 25

Chocolate Cake 26

Chocolate Brownie 27

Cupcakes 28

Crustless Pumpkin Pie 29

Date Slice 30

Fabulous Ginger Crunch 31

Lemon Shortcake 32

Louise Cake 33

Carrot Cake

This is a dairy free recipe if cake is not frosted.

Ingredients:

3 cups carrot (grated)
4 eggs
2 cups soft brown sugar
½ cup oil
1 teaspoon vanilla essence
2 cups **Baking Blend** (p.8)
1 teaspoon guar gum
2 teaspoons baking soda
1 cup raisins
1 cup walnuts (chopped, optional)

Cream Cheese Frosting Ingredients:

50g butter (softened)
150g cream cheese
2 teaspoons lemon juice
2 cups icing sugar

Tip: If using cream cheese frosting the cake should be kept in the fridge.

Frosting Method: Beat all ingredients together. Then spread over the cold cake with a spatula or warm knife.

Sprinkle with toasted pumpkin seeds and chopped dried apricots if desired.

Method:

1. Turn oven on to 160°C fan bake.
2. Line a 30x20cm (12"x8") baking tin with baking paper. Set aside.
3. Grate 3 - 4 carrots on a coarse grater ready to add later.
4. Combine eggs, sugar, oil, vanilla, **Baking Blend**, guar gum and baking soda in a large bowl. Then beat together until uniformly combined.
5. Add raisins, carrots and walnuts (if using), and mix again well.
6. Pour batter into the prepared tin, spreading evenly across the tin.
7. Bake at 160°C fan bake for 50 minutes or until firm in the centre when pressed and a skewer comes out cleanly.
8. Cool on a wire rack. Ice with frosting when cold if using.

Banana Cake

Ingredients:

125g butter (softened)
1 cup sugar
1 egg
1 teaspoon baking soda
3 Tablespoons milk
2 bananas (mashed)
1½ cups **Baking Blend** (p.8)
1 teaspoon guar gum
1½ teaspoons baking powder

Chocolate Frosting Ingredients:

3 Tablespoons cocoa powder
1 Tablespoon boiling water
25g butter (softened)
2 cups icing sugar

Tip: Don't worry if the batter looks all curdled. It'll be fine once baked.

Method:

1. Turn oven on to 170°C fan bake.
2. Line a 20cm (8") square baking tin with baking paper. Set aside.
3. With an electric beater, beat together the butter and sugar until smooth and creamy.
4. Add egg and beat again.
5. In a separate small dish, measure out the baking soda and milk. Stir.
6. Then add to the main bowl the soda/milk mix along with the mashed bananas. Mix well.
7. Now mix in the **Baking Blend**, gum and baking powder.
8. Pour batter into the prepared baking tin.
9. Bake in the middle of the oven at 170°C fan bake for 45 minutes.
10. Remove from oven when cooked and cool on a wire rack. If desired ice when cool.
11. To make frosting measure the cocoa powder into a bowl and pour boiling water over. Stir to dissolve. Add softened butter and icing sugar and mix together until smooth.
12. Spread onto cake using a spatula dipped in hot water. Allow to sit for 10 minutes before cutting the cake.

Moist Fruit Cake

Ingredients:

500g mixed dried fruit
(raisins, sultanas, currants,
cherries, etc.)

250g butter
1 Tablespoon marmalade
(with lots of peel)

3 eggs
1 cup sugar

1½ cups **Baking Blend** (p.8)
1 teaspoon baking powder

Method:

1. Place the dried fruit in a large saucepan. Cover with water and bring to the boil on the stove top and simmer for 10 minutes.
2. Line a 20cm (8") square baking tin with baking paper. Set aside.
3. When the 10 minutes is up, drain the water off the plumped up fruit, and add the diced butter and marmalade. Place a lid on the saucepan and leave while the butter melts through the fruit.
4. Turn the oven on to 180°C fan bake.
5. In a bowl combine the eggs and sugar together then add to cooling fruit in the saucepan. Mix through well.
6. Next add the **Baking Blend** and baking powder.
7. Mix all the ingredients together thoroughly and pour into the prepared tin.
8. Bake at 180°C fan bake for 1 hour.
9. Remove from the oven and leave to cool for 10 - 15 minutes before turning out onto a wire rack to finish cooling.

Christmas Cake

Ingredients:

500 - 750g mixed dried fruit
(raisins, sultanas, currants, cherries, mixed peel, etc.)
250g butter

3 eggs
1 cup soft brown sugar
2 Tablespoons treacle (or molasses)
1 Tablespoon almond essence

1½ cups **Baking Blend** (p.8)
1 teaspoon baking powder
2 teaspoons guar gum
1 teaspoon mixed spice
1 teaspoon cinnamon
1 teaspoon nutmeg

2 Tablespoons sherry or brandy

Method:

1. Place the dried fruits (except cherries and peel) in a large saucepan. Cover with water and bring to the boil on the stove top. Simmer for 10 minutes.
2. Meanwhile prepare a deep 20cm (8") square baking tin by lining with baking paper.
3. When 10 minutes is up, drain water off the plumped fruit, then add the diced butter to the pan. Place a lid on the saucepan and leave for butter to melt through the fruit.
4. Turn the oven on to 180°C fan bake.
5. In a bowl mix together the eggs, sugar, treacle and almond essence then add to cooling fruit in the saucepan. Add the cherries and mixed peel, then stir thoroughly.
6. Next add the dry ingredients and blend all together well, then pour into the prepared tin.
7. Bake at 180°C fan bake for 1 hour.
8. Remove from the oven and leave to cool for 10 - 15 minutes before turning out onto a wire rack to finish cooling.
9. While cake is still warm use a thin skewer to make several holes in the bottom of the cake and pour the brandy evenly over it.
10. Once cold, if desired, ice first with almond icing and then a layer of royal icing.

Chocolate Cake

Ingredients:

125g butter
1 cup sugar
2 Tablespoons golden syrup
½ cup milk
1 teaspoon baking soda
½ cup milk
1 teaspoon vanilla essence
1½ cups **Baking Blend** (p.8)
1 teaspoon guar gum
2 Tablespoons cocoa powder
1 teaspoon ground cinnamon
1 teaspoon mixed spice

Butter Icing Ingredients:

2 Tablespoons of cocoa powder
1 Tablespoon boiling water
25g butter (softened)
1½ cups icing sugar

Method:

1. Turn oven on to 180°C fan bake.
2. Line a 22cm (9") round baking tin with baking paper. Set aside.
3. Melt together in a saucepan the butter, sugar, syrup and milk (it may look curdled, but this is ok and will not affect the cake).
4. In a separate small bowl, measure out the baking soda and second amount of milk. Add vanilla. Stir and set aside.
5. To the saucepan, add the **Baking Blend**, gum, cocoa powder and spices. Mix well.
6. Lastly add the soda/milk mixture. Mix well. (It doesn't need to be entirely smooth).
7. Pour the batter into the prepared baking tin.
8. Bake in the middle of the oven at 180°C fan bake for approximately 30 minutes.
9. Remove from oven when cooked and cool on a wire rack.
10. If desired, once the cake is cold, ice with chocolate butter icing or dust with icing sugar.
11. To make icing put cocoa powder into a bowl and pour boiling water over it. Stir to dissolve. Add softened butter and icing sugar. Mix together till smooth then ice cake.

Chocolate Brownie

Ingredients:

250g butter
½ cup cocoa powder
2 cups sugar
4 eggs
1 teaspoon vanilla essence
1 teaspoon baking powder
2 cups **Baking Blend** (p.8)

Method:

1. Turn oven on to 180°C fan bake.
2. Line a 26cm (10") square tin (or sponge roll tin) with baking paper. Set aside.
3. Melt together in a saucepan butter and cocoa powder, stirring for a couple of minutes.
4. Remove from the heat and stir in sugar.
5. Add eggs one at a time mixing well, until mixture is shiny and well combined.
6. Beat in the vanilla essence.
7. Stir in the **Baking Blend** and baking powder.
8. Pour the batter into the prepared cake tin.
9. Bake at 180°C fan bake for 35 minutes or until a skewer comes out cleanly.
10. Remove from oven but leave in tin for 5 minutes, before transferring to wire rack to cool.
11. When ready to serve lightly dust with icing sugar.

Cupcakes

Ingredients:

125g butter (softened)
½ cup sugar
2 eggs
1 teaspoon vanilla essence
1¼ cups **Baking Blend** (p.8)
1 teaspoon baking powder
1 Tablespoon milk

Frosting Ingredients:

50g butter (softened)
2 cups icing sugar
1 teaspoon vanilla essence
1 - 2 Tablespoons milk
1 - 2 drops food colouring (if desired)

Method:

1. Turn oven on to 180ºC fan bake.
2. Prepare a muffin pan with cupcake paper cases. Set aside.
3. With an electric beater, beat together the butter and sugar until smooth and creamy.
4. Add eggs and vanilla and beat well.
5. Add **Baking Blend**, baking powder and milk then mix until smooth.
6. Half fill paper cases with batter (approx. 1 Tablespoon).
7. Bake at 180ºC fan bake for 15 minutes.
8. Remove from oven and leave for approx. 5 minutes in the pans to firm.
9. Remove cupcakes to a wire rack to cool.
10. While cupcakes cool prepare the frosting by mixing all frosting ingredients together in a small bowl until smooth.
11. Attach desired nozzle to piping bag and fill bag with the frosting.
12. Once cupcakes are cold decorate with creativity and flair!

Tip: Use different coloured frosting, sprinkles, small sweets etc to decorate. These are great for kids parties.

Crustless Pumpkin Pie

This is a dairy free recipe.

Ingredients:

2 cups squash/pumpkin (mashed)
3 eggs
1 cup soft brown sugar
½ teaspoon salt
1 teaspoon cinnamon
1 teaspoon ground ginger
½ teaspoon ground cloves
¾ cup **Baking Blend** (p.8)
1 cup coconut cream

To prepare mashed squash/pumpkin:

- Clean the skin. Cut pumpkin into wedge shaped sections. Remove seeds.
- Microwave, covered, on high until soft, approx. 5 minutes (you can bake in oven if preferred). Cool.
- Scrape flesh from skins and mash with a fork. Add a little water as needed but do not make the mash too runny. It should be a firm mash.
- Measure 2 cups of mashed pumpkin and set aside.

Method:

1. Turn oven on to 180°C fan bake.
2. Beat eggs and brown sugar together with a fork.
3. Add mashed pumpkin and beat again.
4. Add the rest of the ingredients and mix to a thick batter.
5. Pour into a 22 - 24cm **greased** quiche dish or similar sized tin.
6. Bake at 180°C fan bake for 1 hour.
7. Cool in dish and cut when cold. Serve with grated nutmeg sprinkled on top.

Tip: This is an excellent school lunch item if made in paper cases or muffin tins. If making this size then only bake for approx. 25 minutes.

Date Slice

Ingredients:

1 cup dates (chopped)
1 teaspoon baking soda
1 cup boiling water

60g butter
1 cup sugar
1 egg
1 teaspoon vanilla essence
1½ cups **Baking Blend** (p.8)
½ teaspoon guar gum

Lemon Frosting Ingredients:

50g butter (softened)
1 lemon (zest of)
1 Tablespoon lemon juice
2 cups icing sugar

Method:

1. Place roughly chopped dates in a bowl with the baking soda. Pour over the boiling water. Leave to cool.
2. In a large saucepan heat together butter and sugar until all the butter is melted.
3. Remove from stove top and leave to cool.
4. Turn oven on to heat at 160°C fan bake.
5. Line a 20cm (8") square, shallow baking tin with baking paper. Set aside.
6. Add egg and vanilla to the saucepan mixture and beat together. Then add **Baking Blend** and gum.
7. Mash the dates and then add to the rest of the ingredients. Mix together until well combined.
8. Pour into baking tin and bake at 160°C fan bake for 30 minutes.
9. Remove from oven and transfer to a wire rack to cool.
10. While slice is cooling mix together all the frosting ingredients until smooth. Spread frosting over slice. Cut when cold.

Fabulous Ginger Crunch

Ingredients:

125g butter (at room temperature)
½ cup sugar
1¾ cups **Baking Blend** (p.8)
1 teaspoon baking powder
1 teaspoon ground ginger

Topping:

100g butter
1½ cups icing sugar
3 Tablespoons golden syrup
4 teaspoons ground ginger

Method:

1. Turn oven on to 190°C fan bake.
2. Line a 26cm (10") square tin (or sponge roll tin) with baking paper. Set aside.
3. With an electric beater, beat together the butter and sugar until smooth and creamy.
4. Add to the butter and sugar mix the **Baking Blend**, baking powder and ginger. Then mix until it comes together as a crumbly dough.
5. Press firmly and evenly into the prepared tin.
6. Bake at 190°C fan bake for 25 minutes.
7. Meanwhile prepare the topping.
8. In a small saucepan heat the topping ingredients until melted together into a smooth pouring consistency. Don't let it boil as the topping only needs to combine.
9. When the base is cooked, remove from oven and pour the topping over it. Carefully tip the tin so that it reaches all the corners and then place on an even surface to cool.
10. Before slice is completely cold cut into squares with a damp sharp knife.
11. Store in an **airtight** container.

Tip: For a softer "cakey" base add 1 beaten egg after mixing dough together and before putting in tin. Mix well to combine with dough.

Lemon Shortcake

Ingredients:

2 cups **Baking Blend** (p.8)
2 teaspoons baking powder
1 cup castor sugar

125g cold butter
2 eggs
1½ cups lemon honey/curd
⅓ cup **Baking Blend** (p.8)

Method:

1. Turn oven on to 180ºC fan bake.
2. Line a 26cm (10") square tin (or sponge roll tin) with baking paper. Set aside.
3. Place the **Baking Blend**, baking powder and sugar into a food processor.
4. Add the cubed cold butter and whizz until it looks like fine crumbs.
5. Add eggs and mix until the dough comes together.
6. Press half the dough into the tin.
7. Spread lemon honey over the base.
8. Add the other ⅓ cup of baking mix to the remaining dough and whizz until the dough resembles breadcrumbs again.
9. Crumble the dough evenly over the top.
10. Bake at 180ºC fan bake for 35 - 40 minutes until golden brown.
11. Remove from oven and cool in tin for 5 minutes.
12. Remove to a wire rack and when cold, slice and serve dusted with icing sugar.

Tip: Use Christmas Fruit Mince in place of lemon honey for a delicious alternative to Christmas Mince Pies.

You need a food processor to make this recipe.

Louise Cake

Ingredients:

125g soft butter
½ cup castor sugar
2 eggs separated
1 teaspoon vanilla essence
1½ cups **Baking Blend** (p.8)
1 teaspoon guar gum
1½ teaspoons baking powder
Red berry/plum jam

Topping Ingredients:

2 egg whites
⅓ cup castor sugar
1¼ cups coconut

Method:

1. Preheat oven to 170°C fan bake.
2. Line a sponge roll tin 20x23cm (8"x9") with baking paper. Set aside.
3. With an electric beater, beat together the butter and sugar until smooth and creamy.
4. Add the egg yolks and vanilla and beat again.
5. Mix in dry ingredients with a spoon.
6. Press firmly and evenly into the tin.
7. Spread base with jam (berry or plum works well).
8. In a clean bowl beat the egg whites until stiff. (See Lemon Meringue Pie recipe p.63 tip box for beating egg whites).
9. Add the castor sugar slowly while continuing to beat.
10. Mix in the coconut then spread topping over the base right to the edges.
11. Bake at 170°C fan bake for 35 minutes until golden.
12. Allow to cool before removing from tin (keep on baking paper) to a wire rack.
13. When cold, cut into squares and store in **airtight** tin.

Breads

Tips for Bread Baking 36

Pizza Bases 37

Bread Baking for Novice Bakers 38

Basic Bread for Bread Bakers 40

Exseedingly Good Bread 41

Poppyseed Bread 42

Spicy Fruit Bread 43

Hot Cross Buns 44

Recipe for Breadmaker Machine 45

Festive Loaf 46

Quick Flat Bread 47

All the Bread Recipes are Dairy Free and can be made Egg Free too.

Tips for Bread Baking

Maintaining all ingredients at a warm temperature: 40 - 50°C is an ideal temperature range for yeast to grow. Warming the tins and using warm liquids (see detailed recipes) also help this, and cuts down the time taken to produce a lovely loaf. If you are going to use the oven as a warm environment (as suggested in the recipes) yeast preparation times will vary if you use a plastic jug instead of glass or metal.

Use only pure yeast granules (often called Active Dried Yeast): Beware of "bread improver" yeast products often found alongside yeast granules in the supermarket as they are normally NOT gluten free. If you can obtain and prefer to use fresh yeast, adjust the amount of yeast used in the recipes according to the yeast packet instructions.

Why prepare the yeast first instead of combining with the flour? The quality and vigour of yeast varies over time. If you add it to the flour and only find out once it is in the rising stage that it isn't working effectively (i.e. your bread won't rise) you may have just wasted all your other ingredients. So we advise that you follow our method of preparing the yeast separately unless you are very confident of your yeast's raising ability.

Use of molasses: This is a great source of minerals and is a very easily absorbed source of iron. It will also give your loaf of bread a wholesome brown colour. Leave it out if you want a white dough. You can substitute with treacle if molasses isn't available in your area.

Baking tins: Feel free to use whatever tins of any shape and size you have, just be careful to only ½ fill them to leave space for the dough to rise. If using very small tins rising and baking times may need to be adjusted. You may also need to grease your tins before using.

What to do if your loaf rises too near the top of the tin? Using a spatula or spoon, stab the loaf numerous times to let out the air (in effect 'punch down'). Then smooth over the top and leave to rise again - approximately 15 minutes and bake as usual.

Slicing the loaf: Be sure to leave the loaf to fully cool (this can take several hours) before slicing and freezing, otherwise the knife gets sticky, tearing and crumbling the loaf. It's equally important to always use a proper bread knife (finely serrated) to get the best results when slicing.

Keeping your bread: As this bread has no preservatives or additives it will not keep fresh for long so we recommend if it is not all eaten on the day baked, slicing and freezing the bread is the best way to retain its qualities. You can use it slice by slice straight from frozen for toasting (to make sandwiches see next tip). Just remember it will need extra time in the toaster to achieve the usual golden brown toast colour.

Making a successful sandwich from frozen slices of bread:
- First remove slice(s) from the freezer.
- Wrap in a paper towel.
- Microwave for approx. 1 minute on High power for one slice (add about 20 seconds for each extra slice).
- Then use to make your sandwich as you would with fresh bread.

This process seems to steam and refresh the binding qualities of the ingredients in the bread resulting, (in our opinion), in a better sandwich.

Flat breads: Fancy breads such as focaccia or cheesy topped flat breads can be made by using the **Basic Bread Recipe**. Leave to rise for the time listed but bake for only 20 minutes. Remember, without the strength of gluten, the dough will only rise a little on a baking tray as it tends to spread outwards as well. Better results can be obtained by placing the dough in a greased metal dish with shallow sides to give it a shape to mould to.

Buns: Use your favourite **Bread Recipe** to make buns in a 6 mould Texas muffin pan or other small round tins or make rings with stiff baking paper. Rise as usual but cook for only 20 minutes. Alternatively, use rounds of baking paper to separate each bun in a larger tray. You may end up with slightly odd shapes but they still taste great (see Hot Cross Buns recipe p.44 for how to do this).

Pizza bases: The **White Bread Recipe** makes a great pizza base(s), depending on the size and thickness you desire. Remember they will spread both outwards and a little upwards while rising (like flat bread) unless you use a shallow pan. Bake for only 20 minutes. Keep cooked bases in the freezer for a quick meal - just add your favourite toppings.

Bread Baking for Novice Bakers

Ingredients:

1 teaspoon sugar
¼ cup boiling water
½ cup cold water
2 teaspoons active dried yeast

1 cup boiling water
1 Tablespoon molasses (optional)
1 cup cold water
⅓ cup vegetable oil
4 eggs (beaten)

5 cups **Bread Blend** (p.8)
1½ Tablespoons guar gum
1 teaspoon salt

Tip: When mixed together the dough will progress from being sloppy, as the gum is activated, to thick. Don't panic if it looks lumpy at first this will mix out. Be careful to mix right to the bottom of the bowl. Beat until smooth. A few minutes with a hand held beater using dough hooks or a cake mixer using the beater attachment will improve your loaf's texture but is not vital.

Method:

1. Turn oven on to 40 - 50°C fan bake.
2. Boil a kettle of water.
3. Oil two 20x13x9cm (8"x5"x3.5") loaf tins, or one large tin 12x12x23cm. (5"x5"x9")
4. Place sugar in a 500ml glass jug/bowl. Pour over ¼ cup of boiling water and stir to dissolve sugar. Using the same measure, add 2 more ¼ cups of cold water.
5. Sprinkle yeast granules into the jug of water. Place in the oven for approx. 15 minutes to allow the yeast to activate and bubble (it should near the top of the jug when ready).
6. Into a 1litre jug/bowl measure 1 cup of still hot water from the kettle (don't boil it again). Dissolve into this the molasses (if using this healthy option).
7. Add to this a further 1 cup of cold water and the vegetable oil.
8. Break eggs into the jug. Blend together thoroughly using a blender, eggbeater or fork.
9. In a large bowl put the **Bread Blend**, gum and salt and make a well shape in the centre.
10. When yeast is ready add both jugs of liquid ingredients to the **Bread Blend**, stirring together until it becomes thick and sticky and completely combined.
11. Divide evenly into your loaf tins, or a single jumbo tin. Ensure dough is well distributed into the corners.

12. Using a dampened spatula, smooth over the top. Place the loaf tins in the warm oven.
13. Leave to rise until dough nears the top of the tin, approx. 30 - 40 minutes.
14. Remove tins gently, and place on an insulated surface such as a wooden cutting board, place mat or similar, so that the warm loaf doesn't get chilled from a cold surface. The dough will continue to rise while your oven heats but don't let it rise over the top of the tin or you will get large air holes under your crust (see tip p.36 for help if this happens).
15. Turn oven up to 210°C fan bake and when at temperature, bake loaves for 45 minutes.
16. Remove from oven and turn out of tins onto a wire rack to cool. Turn oven off.
17. Slice your delicious bread when completely cold.

Sugar & warm water ready for yeast

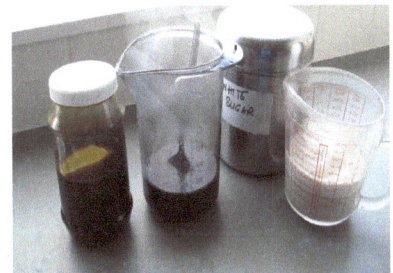
Molasses in hot water. Yeast growing

Add oil to the molasses & water jug

Ready to beat eggs together

Blend molasses, water, oil, eggs

Yeast has risen enough to use

Add all liquids to the flour bowl

Mix together until thick & sticky

Fill tin to half full, smooth top

Risen & now in oven to bake

Deliciously browned

Tip out to cool on wire rack

Basic Bread for Bread Bakers

Ingredients:

1 teaspoon sugar
¾ cup warm water
2 teaspoons active dried yeast

2 cups warm water
1 Tablespoon molasses (optional)
⅓ cup vegetable oil
4 eggs (beaten)

5 cups **Bread Blend** (p.8)
1½ Tablespoons guar gum
1 teaspoon salt

Method:

1. In a 500ml jug or bowl dissolve sugar in warm water.
2. Sprinkle dried yeast over the top, and leave to activate and bubble in a warm place. When ready, it should fill the jug to ¾ full.
3. Meanwhile, blend together molasses with oil.
4. Add water and stir in 4 beaten eggs.
5. Into a large bowl put the **Bread Blend**, gum and salt.
6. Make a well shape in the centre and add both jugs of liquid ingredients stirring together until it becomes thick and sticky. Beating well for 4 minutes (with an electric mixer) will improve the dough.
7. Half fill baking tin(s) ensuring dough is well distributed into the corners.
8. Using a dampened spatula, smooth over the top and leave to rise in a warm place until the dough nears the top of the tin. The dough will continue to rise while the oven heats up so allow for this and don't let it rise over the top of the tin or you will get large air holes under your crust (see tip p.36 for help if this happens).
9. Turn on oven and when hot, bake at 210°C fan bake for 45 minutes.
10. Turn out of tins onto a wire rack to cool. Slice when completely cold.

Exseedingly Good Bread

Ingredients:

1 teaspoon sugar
¾ cup warm water
2 teaspoons active dried yeast

2 cups warm water
1 Tablespoon molasses (optional)
⅓ cup vegetable oil
4 eggs (beaten)

5 cups **Bread Blend** (p.8)
1½ Tablespoons guar gum
1 teaspoon salt
1½ Tablespoons sunflower seeds
1½ Tablespoons pumpkin seeds
1 teaspoon poppy seeds
1 teaspoon flaxseed (linseed)

Tip: Refer to detailed method under Bread Baking for Novice Bakers if required remembering to add seeds of your choice to the dry ingredients bowl.

Method:

1. In a 500ml jug or bowl dissolve sugar in warm water. Sprinkle dried yeast over the top, and leave to activate and bubble in a warm place. When ready, it should fill the jug to ¾ full.
2. Meanwhile, blend together molasses with oil. Add water and stir in 4 beaten eggs.
3. Into a large bowl put the **Bread Blend**, gum, salt and seeds.
4. Make a well shape in the centre and add both jugs of liquid ingredients stirring together until it becomes thick and sticky. Beating well for 4 minutes with an electric mixer will improve the dough.
5. Half fill baking tin(s) ensuring dough is well distributed into the corners.
6. Using a dampened spatula, smooth over the top and leave to rise in a warm place until the dough nears the top of the tin. The dough will continue to rise while the oven heats up so allow for this and don't let it rise over the top of the tin or you will get large air holes under your crust (see tip p.36 for help if this happens).
7. Turn on oven and when hot, bake at 210°C fan bake for 45 minutes.
8. Turn out of tins onto a wire rack to cool. Slice when completely cold.

Poppyseed Bread

Ingredients:

1 teaspoon sugar
¾ cup warm water
2 teaspoons active dried yeast

2 cups warm water
1 Tablespoon molasses (optional)
⅓ cup vegetable oil
4 eggs (beaten)

5 cups **Bread Blend** (p.8)
1½ Tablespoons guar gum
1 teaspoon salt
3 Tablespoons poppy seeds

Tip: Refer to detailed method under Bread Baking for Novice Bakers if required remembering to add poppy seeds to the dry ingredients bowl.

Substituting some of the water with the juice of 1 orange makes a tasty variation to this bread.

Method:

1. In a 500ml jug or bowl dissolve sugar in warm water.
2. Sprinkle dried yeast over the top, and leave to activate and bubble in a warm place. When ready, it should fill the jug to ¾ full.
3. Meanwhile, blend together molasses with oil.
4. Add water and stir in 4 beaten eggs.
5. Into a large bowl put the **Bread Blend**, gum, salt and seeds.
6. Make a well shape in the centre and add both jugs of liquid ingredients stirring together until it becomes thick and sticky. Beating well for 4 minutes with an electric mixer will improve the dough.
7. Half fill baking tin(s) ensuring dough is well distributed into the corners.
8. Using a dampened spatula, smooth over the top and leave to rise in a warm place until the dough nears the top of the tin. The dough will continue to rise while the oven heats up so allow for this and don't let it rise over the top of the tin or you will get large air holes under your crust (see tip p.36 for help if this happens).
9. Turn on oven and when hot, bake at 210°C fan bake for 45 minutes.
10. Turn out of tins onto a wire rack to cool. Slice when completely cold.

Spicy Fruit Bread

Ingredients:

1 teaspoon sugar
¾ cup warm water
2 teaspoons active dried yeast

2 cups warm water
1 Tablespoon molasses (optional)
⅓ cup vegetable oil
4 eggs (beaten)

5 cups **Bread Blend** (p.8)
1½ Tablespoons guar gum
1 teaspoon salt
2 - 3 Tablespoons mixed spice
(or according to taste)
¼ cup raisins
¾ cup currants

Tip: Refer to detailed method under Bread Baking for Novice Bakers if required remembering to add the spices, raisins and currants to the dry ingredients bowl.

Method:

1. In a 500ml jug or bowl dissolve sugar in warm water.
2. Sprinkle dried yeast over the top, and leave to activate and bubble in a warm place. When ready, it should fill the jug to ¾ full.
3. Meanwhile, blend together molasses with oil.
4. Add water and stir in 4 beaten eggs, mix in raisins and currants.
5. Into a large bowl put the **Bread Blend**, gum, salt and spices.
6. Make a well shape in the centre and add both jugs of liquid ingredients stirring together until it becomes thick and sticky. Beating well for 4 minutes with an electric mixer will improve the dough.
7. Half fill baking tin(s) ensuring dough is well distributed into the corners.
8. Using a dampened spatula, smooth over the top and leave to rise in a warm place until the dough nears the top of the tin. The dough will continue to rise while the oven heats up so allow for this and don't let it rise over the top of the tin or you will get large air holes under your crust (see tip p.36 for help if this happens).
9. Turn on oven and when hot, bake at 210°C fan bake for 50 minutes.
10. Turn out of tins onto a wire rack to cool. Slice when completely cold.

Hot Cross Buns

Use Spicy Fruit Bread ingredients p.43 to make the buns.

'Cross' Ingredients:

½ cup rice flour or **Baking Blend** (p.8)
⅓ cup water

Sugar Glaze Ingredients:
1 Tablespoon sugar
1 Tablespoon water

Method:

1. Prepare about 18 - 20 rounds of baking paper approximately 15cm (6") in diameter.
2. Set aside a bowl of water and large baking dish.
3. Follow method steps 1 - 6 in the Spicy Fruit Bread recipe.
4. Dampen hands then scoop a small handful of dough into damp hands and mould to a round shape. Place in the centre of the round of baking paper drawing paper up around the sides and place in square baking dish (a square metal cake tin is good).
5. Repeat step 4 until all the dough is used up, placing the buns a small space apart in the baking dish with the paper between them, to keep them separate.
6. Leave to rise in a warm place such as in your oven at 40°C until nearly doubled in size.
7. Take buns out, if rising in the oven, and turn oven on to 200°C fan bake.
8. Mix 'cross' ingredients together in a small bowl until a smooth paste is formed - like icing. Then place into the corner of a small strong bag. Cut off a small piece of the corner of the bag and then use to pipe 'crosses' onto the buns.
9. Bake at 200°C fan bake for 25 - 30 minutes.
10. Make a sugar glaze for the top of the buns by dissolving sugar in water and microwave on full power for approx. 30 seconds. Be careful this mix will be **very** hot!
11. Remove buns from oven then brush buns with sugar glaze.
12. Leave to cool for 5 minutes before removing from tins and peeling off the baking paper. Then enjoy warm or leave on a wire rack to finish cooling.

Tip: These can be made ahead of time and frozen until needed. To reheat from frozen, wrap 1 bun at a time in a paper towel and microwave for approx. 40 seconds until warm and soft.

Recipe for Breadmaker Machine

Our bread recipes were initially developed without the use of a breadmaker machine as we believe the handmade method, as well as being very simple to do, delivers the best bread loaf. However, we do understand that some people prefer to use a bread machine. So feel free to experiment - but results will vary widely depending on the make and model of breadmaker used. We suggest you keep a close watch on your first attempt to bake a loaf in your machine as variability in yeast or breadmaker settings could cause it to rise over the top of the bread pan making a very big mess! If it rises too much, remove pan and advance breadmaker to the baking cycle then put back in to cook.

> The bread below was made in a machine using the following settings: The gluten free cycle used was for a 1kg (2.2lbs) Loaf (if your machine only makes a smaller loaf we suggest you reduce the ingredient quantities proportionally) = Total Time: 2hr15min
> Total Kneading Time: 20min   1st (and only)Rise: 50min   Bake Time: 65min

Please select the cycle on your breadmaker that matches closest to the above settings. It's very important you **DO NOT** select a cycle that has a "knock down/knead" and 2nd Rise.

Ingredients:

5 cups **Bread Blend** (p.8)
1½ Tablespoons guar gum
1 teaspoon salt
1 teaspoon sugar
1 level teaspoon active dried yeast
1¼ cups hot water
1½ cups cold water
⅓ cup vegetable oil
4 eggs
1 Tablespoon molasses (optional)

Method:

1. Into a large bowl put the **Bread Blend**, gum, salt, sugar and yeast.
2. In a separate bowl first add the hot water (boiled hot from a kettle). Into this put the molasses and stir until dissolved. Add the cold water, then oil and eggs. Blend well.
3. Add the liquid ingredients to the dry ingredients and mix with a large spoon until all the ingredients are well combined (like you would for a cake).
4. Spoon dough into bread pan, pressing down after each spoonful to eliminate any gaps or air bubbles. Make sure the mixing paddle is still upright and lock bread pan into place in the breadmaker.
5. Select the correct cycle for your particular breadmaker. Slice when completely cold.

Festive Loaf

Ingredients:

1 teaspoon sugar
¾ cup warm water
2 teaspoons active dried yeast

1 Tablespoon golden syrup
2 cups warm water
⅓ cup vegetable oil
4 eggs
Almond essence

5 cups **Bread Blend** (p.8)
1½ Tablespoons guar gum
1 teaspoon salt
1½ cups mixed dried fruit (raisins, red and green cherries, currants, peel, etc.)

Method:

1. Follow steps 1 - 7 for Bread Baking for Novice Bakers.
2. Break the eggs into the jug and beat together with the almond essence.
3. In large bowl put the **Bread Blend** and dried fruit. Mix together thoroughly and make a well shape in the centre.
4. When yeast is ready, put all the ingredients into the large bowl, and mix together until it becomes thick and sticky. Beat for a few minutes with an electric beater if desired.
5. With wet hands, take about a ½ cup of dough and "roll" into a ball shape then place into ring or round tin spacing approx. 2cm (½")apart. Repeat until tin is full.
6. Place into oven and leave to rise for 30 - 40 minutes until dough is 1 - 2cm (½") from the top of the tin.
7. Remove tin(s) from oven and turn temperature up to 210ºC fan bake.
8. When oven is up to temperature, bake at 210ºC fan bake for 35 - 40 minutes.
9. Remove from the oven and turn out onto a wire rack to cool.
10. Drizzle with icing, made with ½ cup icing sugar, 2 drops almond essence and a little boiling water. Sprinkle slivered almonds on top.
11. Reheat on Christmas morning in the microwave and break apart to serve.

Tip: Experiment with different shaped tins for baking this sweet bread - a ring tin, round baking tin, small loaf tins or a festive shaped cake tin. Whatever shape takes your fancy.

Quick Flat Bread

Ingredients:

1 cup **Baking Blend** (p.8)
2 teaspoons baking powder
Pinch salt
Pinch pepper (optional)
1 egg
25g butter (melted)
1 cup milk

Variations:
Chopped rosemary and black olives
Chopped basil and dried tomatoes
Grated cheese (best sprinkled on top)

Method:

1. Preheat oven to 175ºC fan bake.
2. Prepare a 20x25cm (approx 8"x10") shallow tin by lining with baking paper.
3. Place **Baking Blend** into a bowl with the baking powder and salt (and pepper if using) and any variations of your choice.
4. Make a well shape in the middle.
5. In a separate bowl/pan melt the butter then add the milk.
6. Next break an egg into the milk and butter mix and beat together with a fork.
7. Add a small amount of the liquids into the dry ingredients bowl and mix quickly together.
8. Continue stirring quickly while gradually adding in the remainder of the liquids.
9. Beat the batter until smooth and pour into the tin, spreading evenly.
10. Bake at 175ºC fan bake for 25 - 30 minutes.
11. Leave to cool in the tin for 10 minutes then transfer to a wire rack to finish cooling.
12. When cold cut into squares to serve.

Tip: Ideal served with soup or as an accompaniment to a light lunch.

Muffins & Scones

Delicious Date Muffins 50

Raspberry & Cream Cheese Muffins 51

Blueberry Muffins 52

Lemon & Poppyseed Muffins 53

Apple & Raisin Muffins 54

Banana Chocolate Chip Muffins 55

Cheese Muffins 56

Savoury Pumpkin Muffins 57

Basic Scones 58

Date Scones 59

Savoury Scones 60

Delicious Date Muffins

Ingredients:

100g butter
1 medium orange (whole, quartered)

½ cup dates
½ cup orange juice
1 egg

1½ cups **Baking Blend** (p.8)
1 teaspoon baking powder
½ cup sugar
1 teaspoon baking soda

Method:

1. Turn oven on to 200°C fan bake.
2. Lightly oil a 12 place muffin pan. Set aside.
3. In a food processor/blender place the butter and the quartered orange (skin and all). Pulse until roughly chopped.
4. Add to this dates, orange juice and egg. Pulse a few times until dates are chopped.
5. In a separate bowl place the remaining dry ingredients.
6. Pour the processor/blender contents into the dry ingredients and mix together until dampened. If a bit dry add a little more orange juice.
7. Divide mixture among the 12 muffin pans.
8. Bake at 200°C fan bake for 15 minutes or until golden and firm to the touch.
9. Leave in the pan for 5 minutes to set before removing to a wire rack to cool.

Tip: If muffin mixture is stirred too much it will not rise well when baking.

Raspberry & Cream Cheese Muffins

Ingredients:

1½ cups **Baking Blend** (p.8)
4 teaspoons baking powder
½ cup castor sugar
½ teaspoon salt

100g butter (melted)
1 cup milk
1 egg

1 cup raspberries (frozen or fresh)

Method:

1. Turn oven on to 210ºC fan bake.
2. Lightly oil a 12 place muffin pan. Set aside.
3. In a bowl place the **Baking Blend**, baking powder, sugar, and salt.
4. Mix through with a fork.
5. In a separate bowl/pan melt the butter then add milk, then egg and mix together well.
6. Gently add the raspberries and liquids to the dry ingredients and mix lightly together only until flour is damp. Do not beat together.
7. Three quarter fill each muffin pan.
8. Bake at 210ºC fan bake for 12 - 15 minutes until golden brown. Cook 3 minutes longer if using frozen raspberries.
9. Remove from oven and cool in tins for 5 minutes.
10. Transfer to a wire rack to finish cooling or serve immediately.

Tip: For a special muffin, put a teaspoon of cream cheese on the top of each one before baking.

Remember, if muffin mixture is stirred too much it will not rise well.

Blueberry Muffins

Ingredients:

1½ cups **Baking Blend** (p.8)
4 teaspoons baking powder
½ cup castor sugar
1 teaspoon cinnamon
½ teaspoon salt
1 cup blueberries (frozen or fresh)

100g butter (melted)
1 cup milk
1 egg

Method:

1. Turn oven on to 210°C fan bake.
2. Lightly oil a 12 place muffin pan. Set aside.
3. In a bowl place **Baking Blend**, baking powder, sugar, cinnamon and salt.
4. Add the blueberries and gently mix through with a fork.
5. In a separate bowl/pan melt the butter then add milk, then egg and mix together well.
6. Add the liquids to the dry ingredients and mix lightly together only until flour is damp. Do not beat together.
7. Three quarter fill each muffin pan.
8. Bake at 210°C fan bake for 12 - 15 minutes until golden brown. If using frozen blueberries, bake for 3 minutes longer.
9. Remove from oven and cool in pan for 5 minutes.
10. Transfer to a wire rack to finish cooling or serve immediately.

Tip: If muffin mixture is stirred too much it will not rise well when baking.

Lemon & Poppyseed Muffins

Ingredients:

1¾ cups **Baking Blend** (p.8)
2 teaspoons baking powder
1 cup sugar
3 Tablespoons poppy seeds
1 lemon (zest of)

100g butter (melted)
1 lemon (juice of)
1 cup milk (approx..)
2 eggs

Method:

1. Turn oven on to 200°C fan bake.
2. Lightly oil a 12 place muffin pan. Set aside.
3. In a bowl place **Baking Blend**, baking powder, sugar and poppy seeds.
4. Add lemon zest. Mix through with a fork.
5. In a separate bowl/pan melt the butter. Add 1 cup total juice/milk mixture (juice 1 lemon into a 1 cup measure and fill to the top with milk). Add eggs and mix together well.
6. Add the liquids to the dry ingredients and mix lightly together only until flour is damp. Do not beat together.
7. Three quarter fill each muffin pan.
8. Bake at 200°C fan bake for 12 - 15 minutes until golden brown.
9. Remove from oven and cool in pan for 3 minutes.
10. Transfer to a wire rack to finish cooling or serve immediately.

Tip: For an extra treat put a ½ teaspoon of lemon honey on top of each muffin before baking.

Remember, if muffin mixture is stirred too much it will not rise well.

Apple & Raisin Muffins

This is a dairy free recipe.

Ingredients:

2 cups **Baking Blend** (p.8)
1 teaspoon guar gum
½ teaspoon baking soda
2 teaspoons baking powder
½ cup brown sugar
½ cup raisins
¼ teaspoon ground cloves
¼ teaspoon cinnamon

1 medium sized apple
¼ cup oil
2 eggs
¼ cup orange juice

Method:

1. Turn oven on to 200ºC fan bake.
2. Lightly oil a 12 place muffin pan. Set aside.
3. Place all the dry ingredients, (**Baking Blend**, gum, soda, baking powder, sugar, raisins & spices) in a large bowl and mix together well.
4. Finely grate unpeeled apple and place in another bowl with oil, eggs and orange juice. Whisk together.
5. Add the liquids to the dry ingredients and mix lightly together only until flour is damp. Do not beat together. Add a little more orange juice if looking too dry.
6. Divide evenly among the 12 muffin pans.
7. Bake at 200ºC fan bake for 12 - 15 minutes or until golden and firm in the centre when pressed.
8. Remove from oven and cool in the pan for 5 minutes.
9. Transfer to a wire rack to finish cooling or serve immediately.

Tip: If muffin mixture is stirred too much it will not rise well when baking.

Banana Chocolate Chip Muffins

Ingredients:

2 cups **Baking Blend** (p.8)
2 teaspoons baking powder
½ cup castor sugar
½ teaspoon salt
½ cup chocolate chips

100g butter (melted)
1 cup milk
1 egg
1 teaspoon vanilla essence
1 cup bananas (2 - 3 mashed bananas)

Method:

1. Turn oven on to 220°C fan bake.
2. Lightly oil a 12 place muffin pan. Set aside.
3. In a bowl place the **Baking Blend**, baking powder, sugar, salt and chocolate chips.
4. Mix through with a fork.
5. Melt the butter in a separate jug/saucepan. Add milk, then eggs and vanilla and mix together well.
6. Stir the mashed banana into the liquid ingredients.
7. Add the liquids to the dry ingredients and mix lightly together only until flour is damp. Do not beat together.
8. Three quarter fill muffin pans.
9. Bake at 220°C fan bake for 12 - 15 minutes until golden brown.
10. Remove from oven and cool in pan for 5 minutes.
11. Transfer to a wire rack to finish cooling or serve immediately.

Tip: If muffin mixture is stirred too much it will not rise well when baking.

Cheese Muffins

Ingredients:

1½ cups **Baking Blend** (p.8)
4 teaspoons baking powder
½ teaspoon salt
1½ cups cheddar cheese (grated)

1 cup milk
2 eggs
⅓ cup red capsicum/pepper (diced)

⅓ cup cheddar cheese (grated, optional)

Method:

1. Turn oven on to 210°C fan bake.
2. Lightly oil a 12 place muffin pan. Set aside.
3. In a bowl place the **Baking Blend**, baking powder and salt.
4. Add first measure of grated cheese. Mix through with a fork.
5. In a smaller bowl mix the milk and eggs together with a fork.
6. Add the diced capsicum/pepper.
7. Add the liquids to the dry ingredients and mix lightly together only until flour is damp. Do not beat together.
8. Three quarter fill muffin pans.
9. Sprinkle second measure of cheese over muffins.
10. Bake at 210°C fan bake for 12 - 15 minutes until golden brown.
11. Remove from oven and cool in pan for 5 minutes.
12. Transfer to a wire rack to finish cooling or serve immediately.

Tip: If muffin mixture is stirred too much it will not rise well when baking.

Savoury Pumpkin Muffins

Ingredients:

1½ cups **Baking Blend** (p.8)
2 teaspoons baking powder
1 Tablespoon sugar
½ teaspoon salt
1 cup cheddar cheese (grated)
2 - 3 Tablespoons fresh herbs (oregano, chives, marjoram etc.)

75g butter (melted)
1 cup milk
1 egg
1 cup pumpkin/squash (cooked and mashed, see method p.29)

Method:

1. Turn oven on to 210ºC fan bake.
2. Lightly oil a 12 place muffin pan. Set aside.
3. In a bowl place the **Baking Blend**, baking powder, sugar, salt, cheese and chopped herbs.
4. Mix through with a fork.
5. In a separate bowl/pan melt the butter then add milk, then egg and mashed pumpkin then mix together well.
6. Add the liquids to the dry ingredients and mix lightly together only until flour is damp. Do not beat together.
7. Three quarter fill each muffin pan.
8. Bake at 210ºC fan bake for 12 - 15 minutes until golden brown.
9. Remove from oven and cool in pan for 5 minutes.
10. Transfer to a wire rack to finish cooling or serve immediately.

Tip: If muffin mixture is stirred too much it will not rise well when baking.

Basic Scones

This can be made dairy free.

Ingredients:

1 rounded cup **Baking Blend** (p.8)
1 teaspoon guar gum

1 teaspoon oil
1 cup milk/whey/buttermilk/water
2 teaspoons baking powder

Method:

1. Turn oven on to 230°C fan bake.
2. Place **Baking Blend** and gum in a bowl.
3. Mix through with a serving spoon, then make a well shape in the centre.
4. Put oil into a measuring cup then fill up to the 1 cup mark with milk (or water for dairy free option).
5. Pour into the well in the **Baking Blend** and mix lightly to form a soft damp dough.
6. Add the baking powder and mix through evenly.
7. Working quickly, take a serving spoon scoop of dough and smooth top with a damp hand.
8. Scrape with a spatula onto an unfloured, ungreased baking tray.
9. Repeat steps 7 and 8 until all dough is used up.
10. Bake at 230°C fan bake for 12 - 15 minutes until golden brown.
11. Remove from oven and place on a wire rack to cool.

Tip: This recipe can be used to make griddle scones on the stove top in a frying pan with a lid on using a medium heat. Remove lid for last 3 minutes. (If you don't have a lid turn scones over after 8 min and cook for remaining time).

This recipe also makes a fantastic quick pizza base.

Date Scones

This can be made dairy free.

Ingredients:

1 rounded cup **Baking Blend** (p.8)
1 teaspoon guar gum
16 dates (cut in half crosswise)

1 teaspoon oil
1 cup milk/whey/buttermilk/water
2 teaspoons baking powder

Method:

1. Turn oven on to 230°C fan bake.
2. Place **Baking Blend**, gum and dates in a bowl.
3. Mix through with a serving spoon, then make a well shape in the centre.
4. Put oil into a measuring cup then fill up to the 1 cup mark with milk (or water for dairy free option).
5. Pour into the well in the flour and mix lightly to form a soft damp dough.
6. Add baking powder and mix through evenly.
7. Working quickly, take a serving spoon scoop of dough and smooth top with a damp hand.
8. Scrape with a spatula onto an unfloured, ungreased baking tray.
9. Repeat steps 7 and 8 until all dough is used up.
10. Bake at 230°C fan bake for 12 - 15 minutes until golden brown.
11. Remove from oven and place on a wire rack to cool.

Tip: This recipe can be used to make griddle scones on the stove top in a frying pan with a lid on, using medium heat. Remove lid for last 3 minutes.

Savoury Scones

Ingredients:

1 rounded cup **Baking Blend** (p.8)
2 teaspoons baking powder
⅓ cup grated carrot
½ cup grated cheddar cheese
½ teaspoon parsley
¼ cup chopped onion

¼ cup milk, whey or buttermilk
1 egg

½ cup grated cheddar cheese

Method:

1. Turn oven on to 230°C fan bake.
2. Place dry ingredients in a bowl along with the carrot, onion, parsley and first measure of grated cheese.
3. Mix through with a serving spoon, then make a well shape in the centre.
4. In another small bowl, lightly beat together the egg and milk.
5. Pour into the well in the flour and mix lightly to form a soft damp dough.
6. Working quickly, take a serving spoon scoop of dough and scrape with a spatula onto an unfloured, ungreased baking tray.
7. Repeat step 6 until all dough is used up.
8. Sprinkle remaining cheese on top of scones.
9. Bake at 230°C fan bake for 12 - 15 minutes until golden brown.
10. Remove from oven and place on a wire rack to cool.

Tip: This recipe can be used to make griddle scones on the stove top in a frying pan with a lid on, using medium heat. Remove lid for last 3 minutes.

Pastry, Pikelets & Pancakes

Sweet Short Pastry 62

Lemon Meringue Pie 63

Fruit & Custard Tarts 64

Neenish Tarts 65

Christmas Mince Pies 66

Savoury Pie Pastry 67

Family Mince Pie 68

Bacon & Egg Pie 69

Savoury Short Pastry 70

Quiche Lorraine 71

Pumpkin Pie 72

Brandy Snaps 73

Crêpes (Pancakes) 74

Pikelets (American Style Pancakes) 75

Waffles 76

Sweet Short Pastry

Ingredients:

1½ cups **Baking Blend** (p.8)
1 teaspoon guar gum
Pinch salt
1 teaspoon baking powder
1 Tablespoon sugar
125g butter (cold)
1 egg yolk beaten with
2 Tablespoons fridge-cold water

Method for Pie Case:

1. Place **Baking Blend**, gum, salt, baking powder and sugar into a medium sized bowl and mix well to evenly distribute the ingredients.
2. Grate the cold butter into the flour. Mix through using a table knife.
3. Separate into small bowls the egg yolk from the white (save the white for use in other recipes).
4. Mix the egg yolk and cold water together with a fork then add to other ingredients. Stir with the knife. It will look very lumpy and lots of ingredients remain dry.
5. Tip out onto a clean dry work surface. Then gather and press dough lumps together until they form a smooth ball.
6. When ready to prepare for baking, turn oven on to 200°C fan bake.
7. Coat a rolling pin and benchtop with flour. Gently begin to roll out the pastry. Turn and roll, turn and roll until approx. 6mm thick all over, and slightly bigger than your pie dish.
8. Next ease the rolling pin under the edge of the pastry until about half way, then lift over pie dish. Ease pastry into the dish and press gently down into the corners.
9. Trim edges and use to patch up holes if they have occurred. Prick base with a fork in several places.
10. Bake at 200°C fan bake for 15 - 20 minutes then leave to cool in the tin.

Tip: Pastry is temperature sensitive. If it gets too warm the butter will melt out and it gets too greasy to roll. If it gets too cold the pastry will crack when rolling. Depending on the climate where you live you may need to put it in the fridge to chill a little. If so wrap in plastic first (it can keep in the fridge for a few days if using later).

Lemon Meringue Pie

Use 1 x Sweet Short Pastry recipe p.62 for the pie case.

Filling Ingredients:

1 cup sugar
4 Tablespoons cornflour*
2 lemons (juice and zest/rind)
3 egg yolks (keep whites aside for topping)
1 cup water
1 Tablespoon butter (softened)

Topping Ingredients:

4 egg whites (this includes the egg white left over from making the pastry case)
½ cup castor sugar
1 teaspoon vanilla

Tip: When beating egg whites the bowl must be completely free from grease, soap residue and absolutely no egg yolk or the whites will not form stiff peaks.

*Use white cornflour/corn starch here, the sort used for thickening sauces.

Method:

Filling:
1. In a microwave proof jug, place the sugar, cornflour and lemon zest/rind. Mix to a smooth paste with the lemon juice.
2. Mix in the egg yolks, water and lastly, butter.
3. Microwave on high for 30 seconds, stir well.
4. Repeat step 3, stirring in between, until a smooth thick mixture is made.
5. Leave to cool down then pour into the cold pastry case to set.

Topping:
1. Beat egg whites in a clean bowl until stiff.
2. Gradually beat in the sugar, a little at a time, until the mixture looks glossy then add vanilla and mix.
3. Spread meringue over the pie being careful to reach all the edges to seal the lemon inside. Make what ever pattern you like on the top.
4. Bake at 200°C fan bake for 10 - 15 minutes or until golden brown.
5. Cool before serving.

Fruit & Custard Tarts

Use 1 x Sweet Short Pastry recipe p.62 for the pie case.

Filling Ingredients:

3 - 4 cups thick custard
Fruit of your choice (fresh or canned)

1 Tablespoon sugar
1 Tablespoon water

Method:

1. Make Sweet Short Pastry.
2. When ready to prepare for baking, turn oven on to 200°C fan bake.
3. If making individual tarts divide pastry before rolling, then roll out with a floured rolling pin on a lightly floured surface.
4. Roll and turn repeatedly until pastry is slightly larger than your flan dish. The dish should be approximately 20cm or 8" diameter if making one large tart.
5. Ease the rolling pin under the edge of the pastry until about half way, then lift over pie dish. Ease pastry into the dish and press gently down into the corners.
6. Prick the base(s) with a fork in several places.
7. Bake at 200°C fan bake for 15 - 20 minutes then leave to cool in tin.
8. When cool ¾ fill tart(s) with custard.
9. Chill until set firm.
10. Then arrange the well-drained canned or fresh fruit of your choice in a nice design on top of the custard.
11. Make glaze by microwaving the sugar and water together (30 seconds maximum – stay and watch).
12. Then brush glaze over the fruit, careful it will be super **hot** and could burn your skin.
13. Chill until ready to serve.

Tip: This makes 1 large tart or 3 - 4 individual tarts.

Neenish Tarts

Ingredients:

125g butter (softened)
½ cup sugar
1 egg
2 cups **Baking Blend** (p.8)
1 teaspoon baking powder
1 teaspoon guar gum
Big pinch salt

Filling Ingredients:

100g butter (softened)
1 cup icing sugar
½ cup sweetened condensed milk
1 medium sized lemon (juice of)

Tip: Icing Ingredients: 2 cups icing sugar, 2 teaspoons cocoa powder and a little boiled water. Or to be quite decadent, use melted white and dark chocolate instead.

Method:

1. Preheat oven to 160°C fan bake.
2. With an electric beater, beat together the butter and sugar until light and fluffy.
3. Add the egg and beat well.
4. Mix in dry ingredients using a spoon, then tip out onto a clean, dry work surface, gather and press dough lumps together until they form a smooth ball.
5. Lightly flour both bench top and rolling pin, take a small golf ball sized piece of the pastry and roll out until about 6mm thick. Place in patty pan. Trim edges. Or use a circular cutter of the right size to cut pastry out and place in patty pan.
6. Repeat until all the dough is used up. Prick the bottom of each tart with a fork.
7. Bake at 160°C fan bake for 12 - 15 minutes or until golden.
8. Leave to cool in the tins for 5 minutes then remove to finish cooling on a wire rack.

Filling & Icing:

1. Blend filling ingredients together and fill tarts evenly. Allow to set.
2. Make white icing with 1 cup icing sugar adding boiling water drop by drop till you get a soft icing consistency. For chocolate icing mix 2 teaspoons cocoa powder with 1 teaspoon boiling water till dissolved then add 1 cup of icing sugar to it. Mix well. Add a few drops of boiling water if needed to get the right consistency.
3. Ice tarts half and half with the 2 icings, let set, then store in an **airtight** tin.

Christmas Mince Pies

Use 1 x Sweet Short Pastry recipe p.62 for the pie cases.

Filling Ingredients:

2 Tablespoons marmalade
2 Tablespoons soft brown sugar
1 apple (grated)
1 Tablespoon lemon juice
½ cup sultanas x 2
½ cup raisins x 2
½ teaspoon salt
½ teaspoon each ground cinnamon, mixed spice, ground cloves, grated nutmeg
1 Tablespoon brandy, sherry or rum

Method:

A few days before baking:
1. Make the fruit mince. Using a stick blender or whizz blend all the ingredients together, using the first measure of dried fruit, till quite smooth.
2. Add the second measure of fruits and blend/pulse briefly so just chopped. Put into clean glass jar(s) with metal screw lids.
3. Store in the fridge so flavours can develop.
4. Prepare Sweet Short Pastry.

On baking day:
1. Turn oven on to 180°C fan bake.
2. Roll out pastry to 5 - 6mm depth. Cut out 12 circles with a cookie cutter large enough that the pastry fits the base and sides of your patty pans.
3. Press each pastry circle carefully down into the patty pans.
4. Fill each pastry case with a spoonful of fruit mince. Cut out 12 circles (or stars) with smaller cookie cutter to make the lids. Press into place.
5. Bake at 180°C fan bake for 15 minutes.
6. Leave to cool in the tins for 5 minutes then remove to finish cooling on a wire rack.
7. Dust with icing sugar to serve.

Savoury Pie Pastry

Ingredients:

2 cups **Baking Blend** (p.8)
175g butter (cold)
2 teaspoons guar gum
Pinch salt
¾ cup fridge-cold water

Method:

1. Place **Baking Blend,** guar gum and salt into a large mixing bowl and mix to distribute evenly.
2. Grate cold butter into the flour. Mix through using a table knife.
3. Add only as much cold water to the pastry mix as needed to make a crumbly dough. It's better to have too little than too much liquid.
4. Tip out onto a clean, dry work surface. Gather and press dough lumps together until they form a smooth ball.
5. If needing a top and bottom for a pie, separate the dough into two pieces, wrap with plastic and place in fridge to rest for 10 minutes if needed (see p.62 for tip about pastry temperature).
6. When ready to prepare for baking, turn oven on to 200°C fan bake. Remove pastry from the plastic bag onto a lightly floured surface, and gently roll with a floured rolling pin. Turn and roll, turn and roll to get an even 3 - 4mm thickness.
7. When you have a piece the right thickness and a bit bigger than your pie dish ease the rolling pin under the edge of the pastry until about half way, then lift over pie dish. Ease pastry into the dish and press gently down into the corners.
8. Roll out the second ball of pastry as above. Place filling of your choice into pie base.
9. Dampen the edges of the pie base with egg wash made from 1 beaten egg and 1 Tablespoon of water.
10. Lift the pastry top into place. Press down at the edges with a fork. Trim extra pastry from the edges. Using a fork, prick the pie top in a few places to let the steam out.
11. Brush all over the pastry top with remaining egg wash.
12. Bake at 200°C fan bake for 30 minutes.
13. Allow to rest for 5 minutes before cutting if serving hot, or allow to cool then refrigerate.

Family Mince Pie

Use 1 x Savoury Pie Pastry recipe p.67 for the pie case.

Filling Ingredients:

400g beef mince (ground beef)
1 onion (sliced)
3 carrots
1 teaspoon beef stock powder
Salt and pepper to taste
1 cup frozen peas
1 Tablespoon **Baking Blend** (p.8)
1 Tablespoon water

Method:

1. In a large frying pan, fry the mince and onion, until the mince is browned and the onions are soft.
2. Dice carrots and add to frying pan with beef stock adding enough water to cover contents.
3. Simmer for 15 minutes then add frozen peas.
4. In a small bowl/cup mix the **Baking Blend** with the water until dissolved then add to frying pan, stirring till the savoury mince mixture thickens.
5. Turn oven to 200°C fan bake and while it heats up prepare your Savoury Pie Pastry.
6. Once frying pan mixture has thickened, pour into prepared pastry case. Dampen edges of pastry with water and place pastry top over the pie. Press edges together with a fork and trim off excess pastry. Prick top several times to let steam escape when it bakes, so pastry won't get soggy.
7. Brush with beaten egg if you want a glazed finish.
8. Bake at 200°C fan bake for 30 minutes.

Tip: A pie is a great way to use up beef or chicken casserole leftovers. The pie filling variations are endless. Have fun experimenting adding garlic or seasonal vegetables.

Tip: New Zealand Classics. For a mince and cheese pie sprinkle 1 cup grated cheddar cheese over the mince before adding pastry top.
For a potato top pie replace the pie pastry top with mashed potato then bake.

Bacon & Egg Pie

Use 1 x Savoury Pie Pastry recipe p.67 for the pie case.

Filling Ingredients:

1 onion
6 rashers of bacon
6 eggs
Chopped fresh herbs (optional)

Method:

1. Make Savoury Pie Pastry.
2. When ready to prepare for baking, turn oven on to 200°C fan bake.
3. On a lightly floured surface, roll out two thirds of the pastry to 4mm thickness and cover the base and sides of a 20cm (8") square pie dish.
4. Sprinkle chopped bacon rashers over the base.
5. Slice the onion and evenly distribute over the bacon with the herbs if using them.
6. Carefully break eggs into the pie dish, no need to mix them up.
7. Dampen the edges of the pastry in the base. You can brush with the egg white remains from egg shells or water.
8. Roll out the remaining pastry and gently place on top of the pie and press the edges together.
9. Bake at 200°C fan bake for 30 minutes.
10. Best eaten cold. Let cool down before slicing.

Tip: This pie is great for picnics. It can be made the day before and kept in the fridge until needed.

Savoury Short Pastry

This can be an egg free pastry.

Ingredients:

1½ cups **Baking Blend** (p.8)
1 teaspoon guar gum
Pinch salt
150g butter (cold)
1 egg
2 Tablespoons fridge-cold water

Method:

1. Place 1 cup of **Baking Blend** and gum into a mixing bowl.
2. Grate the butter into the flour sprinkling the other half cup of flour over the grated butter as you work. (This keeps the butter separated). Once all the butter is grated in, mix through the flour until evenly distributed.
3. In a small bowl/cup place the water and break the egg into it. Whisk together with a fork.
4. Add this to the flour in small amounts mixing as you work, until the mix comes together in coarse lumps.
5. Tip out onto a clean bench and press and roll together until a firm pastry ball is formed (see photo).
6. The pastry can be refrigerated (see p.62 for a tip about pastry temperature) but will work best if returned to room temperature prior to rolling out.
7. Roll out to approx. 5mm thickness on a lightly floured flat surface or between two sheets of baking paper. For ease of use when baking single serve pies, cut the big ball of pastry into smaller pieces and roll each piece out separately.
8. Transfer to your baking dish(es), press gently down into the corners and then trim edges.

Tip: You can substitute the egg in this pastry by grinding 1 Tablespoon of whole flaxseed to a powder then pour over this 3 Tablespoons of boiling water. Leave for approx. 15 minutes to activate then chill in fridge before using in the pastry.

Quiche Lorraine

Use 1 x Savoury Short Pastry recipe p.70 for the quiche case.

Filling Ingredients:

1 - 2 cups chicken, bacon, ham pieces, fish flakes etc (use your imagination or leftovers here)
1 cup cheddar cheese (grated)
1 onion (diced)
1 courgette/zucchini or bell pepper (diced)
1 Tablespoon chopped herbs (optional)
½ cup milk
4 eggs
Salt and pepper to taste

Tip: Use leftovers to make up the first 1-2 cups of ingredients or concoct your own blend of ingredients as all sorts of combinations taste fantastic in a quiche.

Method:

1. Make Savoury Short Pastry.
2. Turn oven on to 200°C fan bake.
3. Roll out pastry to approximately 5mm thickness on a lightly floured flat surface or between two sheets of baking paper. Transfer to 20 - 22cm flan/quiche dish or divide pastry into 3 - 4 smaller balls and roll out and transfer to individual quiche dishes to make single serve quiches. Trim edges.
4. Sprinkle the first four (or five if using herbs) ingredients evenly over the pastry base.
5. In a bowl mix together the milk, eggs, salt and pepper and pour over the quiche.
6. Bake at 200°C fan bake for 30 minutes on a rack in the middle of the oven.
7. Serve either hot or cold. Can be kept in the fridge for a day or two or frozen for later use. Great lunchbox item or for picnics.

Pumpkin Pie

Use 1 x Savoury Short Pastry recipe p.70 for the pie case.

Filling Ingredients:

2 cups squash/pumpkin (mashed)
3 eggs
1 cup soft brown sugar
½ teaspoon salt
1 teaspoon cinnamon
1 teaspoon ground ginger
½ teaspoon ground cloves
1 cup coconut cream

Tip: See p.29 for how to prepare mashed pumpkin. P.29 also has a crustless pumpkin pie recipe.

Method:

1. Make Savoury Short Pastry.
2. Prepare mashed squash/pumpkin. Measure 2 cups of pumpkin and set aside.
3. Turn oven on to 180°C fan bake.
4. Roll out pastry to fit pie dish. Trim edges.
5. In a bowl, beat eggs and brown sugar together with a fork.
6. Add pumpkin and beat again.
7. Add the rest of the ingredients and mix thoroughly through the thick batter.
8. Pour mix into the prepared pastry case.
9. Bake at 180°C fan bake for 1 hour.
10. Leave to cool in dish, cut when cold. Serve with whipped cream or yoghurt and grated nutmeg.

Brandy Snaps or Baskets

Ingredients:

1 Tablespoon golden syrup
25g butter
2 Tablespoons sugar
3 Tablespoons **Baking Blend** (p.8)
½ teaspoon ground ginger

Method:

1. Turn oven on to 150°C fan bake.
2. Wipe baking tray with cooking oil using a paper towel. Also oil an upside down muffin tray if making baskets.
3. In a small saucepan place the butter, sugar and golden syrup.
4. Heat gently until melted and bubbling. Cool.
5. Once cool add **Baking Blend** and ginger and mix through.
6. Place 6 teaspoonful lots on an oiled baking tray allowing plenty of room for the mixture to spread.
7. Bake at 150°C fan bake for 10 minutes.
8. Remove from oven and leave to cool for approx. 1 minute before attempting to remove them from the tray.
9. Working quickly, gently lift each one from the tray with a spatula and if making brandy snaps roll around the handle of a wooden spoon and set aside, or mould over the outside of the muffin tray, fluting with your fingers to make baskets.
10. Leave to cool. Store in an **airtight** container (not plastic) until ready to use.
11. Fill just prior to serving.

Tip: If making brandy snaps have several wooden spoons available to let each snap set a little before removing from the handle.

Crêpes
(Pancakes)

Ingredients:

2 eggs
1 cup **Baking Blend** (p.8)
Pinch salt
1 Tablespoon butter (melted)
1½ cups milk

Dairy Free Ingredients:

2 eggs
1 cup **Baking Blend** (p.8)
Pinch salt
½ cup coconut cream
1 cup water

Method:

1. Break eggs into a bowl or jug.
2. Add **Baking Blend**, salt, butter and milk.

If making Dairy Free, at step 2 use **Baking Blend**, salt, coconut cream and water.

3. Beat until smooth, and let stand for 15 minutes.
4. Cook in ⅓ cup amounts in 25cm nonstick omelette or frying pan turning and tilting the pan as you pour to spread thinly.
5. Allow to cook until edges start to curl up then turn over. (Toss if feeling adventurous). Cook briefly on second side.
6. Remove from pan. Repeat steps 4 - 6 until all batter is used up.

Tip: This recipe works best using a coconut cream that has a content of more than 50% coconut cream listed. Coconut milk or "lite" products are not recommended.

Pikelets

(American Style Pancakes)

Ingredients:

1 egg
2 Tablespoons sugar
1 cup **Baking Blend** (p.8)
Pinch salt
¾ cup milk

1 teaspoon cream of tartar
½ teaspoon baking soda

Method:

1. Put a nonstick frying pan or skillet on to the stove top on a medium heat setting.
2. In a bowl, beat together the egg and sugar.
3. Add **Baking Blend**, and salt.
4. Add milk and mix together until smooth.
5. Prepare a clean folded tea towel handy to your work area for cooked pikelets.
6. At the last minute sift into the batter cream of tartar and baking soda.
7. Mix quickly and thoroughly.
8. Cook in Tablespoon lots in a nonstick frying pan.
9. When the bubbles that appear pop and don't fill in again, turn over (about 20 - 30 seconds).
10. Cook on second side for same amount of time.
11. Remove and place between folded tea towel to cool.
12. Repeat steps 8 - 11 until all batter is used up.

Tip: For American Style Pancakes you can add blueberries or banana or other extras to the batter just make sure they are dry ingredients e.g. tinned fruit won't work very well.

Waffles

Ingredients:

2 egg yolks
1 teaspoon sugar
¾ cup water
½ cup milk
1 teaspoon vanilla essence
80g butter (melted)
2 cups **Baking Blend** (p.8)
Pinch salt
2 teaspoons baking powder

2 egg whites

Method:

1. Separate egg yolks from egg whites and put into separate bowls. Set whites aside.
2. Beat egg yolks with sugar, then mix in water, milk, vanilla and melted butter.
3. Add **Baking Blend**, salt, baking powder and beat together well.
4. Cover and rest for a minimum of 15 minutes.
5. Preheat waffle maker to a ¾ or higher temperature setting.
6. Beat together egg whites until stiff.
7. Fold egg whites carefully into waffle batter. (Do not beat.)
8. When waffle maker has reached temperature, pour approximately ⅓ to ½ cup amount of batter onto waffle iron.
9. Close lid and cook for 3 - 4 minutes.
10. Cool on a wire rack if not serving immediately.

Tip: If making waffles for breakfast, the batter can be prepared the night before, but leave out the baking powder and egg whites adding these just before you want to use the mix in the morning.

Notes

About the Authors

Mary & Vanessa Hudson are a mother and daughter team whose family first encountered the need to eat gluten free because of a Coeliac diagnosis more than 12 years ago, and the subsequent discovery that in fact three quarters of their family were affected with varying degrees of gluten intolerance. They briefly entertained the idea of a lifetime of denial and avoidance of gluten containing foods, but being foodies at heart who loved baking they were not content to simply give up eating the things they had once enjoyed. So they embarked on a quest to create delicious, satisfying, gluten free baked goods that are as much of a joy to cook as they are to eat. Initially they established their company Goodness Me to sell their gluten free bread and baking mixes made according to their secret family recipe, but over the next few years they developed so many tasty recipes that they decided writing a cookbook was the best way to share their secrets. This Gourmand Award winning **Goodness Me it's Gluten Free** Cookbook is the result.

Recipe Index

Afghan Cookies	17
Apple & Raisin Muffins	54
Bacon & Egg Pie	69
Baking Blend	8
Banana Cake	23
Banana Chocolate Chip Muffins	55
Basic Bread for Bread Bakers	40
Basic Scones	58
Blueberry Muffins	52
Brandy Baskets	73
Brandy Snaps	73
Bread Baking for Novice Bakers	38
Bread Baking, Tips for	36
Bread Blend	8
Breadmaker Machine, Recipe for	45
Carrot Cake	22
Cheese Muffins	56
Cherry & Coconut Cookies	14
Chocolate Brownie	27
Chocolate Cake	26
Chocolate Chip Cookies, Irresistible	12
Coconut Crunch Cookies	16
Christmas Cake	25
Christmas Mince Pies	66
Cranberry Cookies	15
Crêpes (Pancakes)	74
Crustless Pumpkin Pie	29
Cupcakes	28
Dainty Biscuits	13
Date Scones	59
Date Slice	30
Delicious Date Muffins	50
Exseedingly Good Bread	41
Fabulous Ginger Crunch	31
Family Mince Pie	68
Festive Loaf	46
Fruit & Custard Tarts	64
Fruit Bread, Spicy	43

Fruit Cake, Moist	24
Ginger Crunch, Fabulous	31
Gingernutty Cookies	18
Hot Cross Buns	44
Irresistible Chocolate Chip Cookies	12
Lemon & Poppyseed Muffins	53
Lemon Meringue Pie	63
Lemon Shortcake	32
Louise Cake	33
Moist Fruit Cake	24
Neenish Tarts	65
Oodles Cookies	19
Pastry, Savoury Pie	67
Pastry, Savoury Short	70
Pastry, Sweet Short	62
Pikelets (American Style Pancakes)	75
Pizza Bases	37
Poppyseed Bread	42
Pumpkin Pie	72
Pumpkin Pie, Crustless	29
Quiche Lorraine	71
Quick Flat Bread	47
Quick Pizza Base (Scone Dough)	58
Raspberry & Cream Cheese Muffins	51
Recipe for Breadmaker Machine	45
Savoury Pie Pastry	67
Savoury Pumpkin Muffins	57
Savoury Scones	60
Savoury Short Pastry	70
Scones, Basic	58
Scones, Date	59
Scones, Savoury	60
Shortcake, Lemon	32
Spicy Fruit Bread	43
Sweet Short Pastry	62
Tips for Bread Baking	36
Waffles	76
Walnut Creams	20

www.ingramcontent.com/pod-product-compliance
Lightning Source LLC
Chambersburg PA
CBHW041157290426
44108CB00003B/92